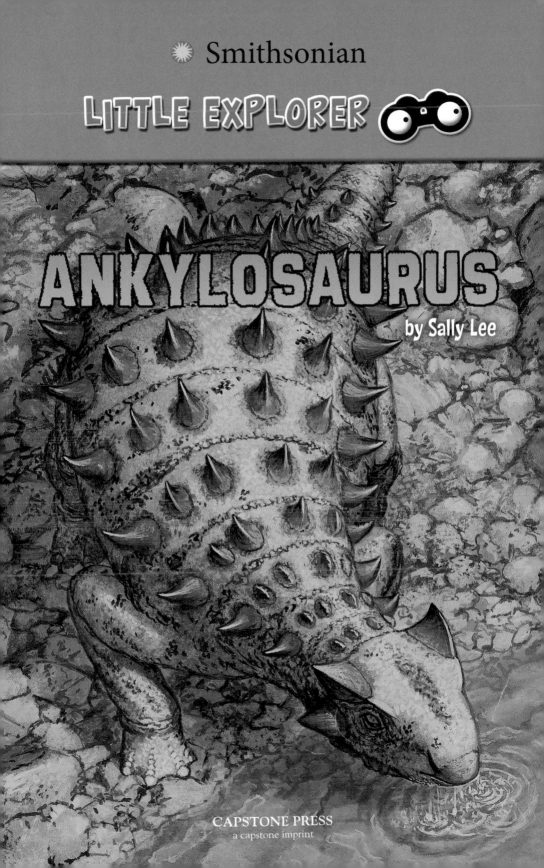

Smithsonian

LITTLE EXPLORER

ANKYLOSAURUS

by Sally Lee

CAPSTONE PRESS
a capstone imprint

Little Explorer is published by Capstone Press,
1710 Roe Crest Drive, North Mankato, Minnesota 56003
www.capstoneyoungreaders.com

Library of Congress Cataloging-in-Publication Data

Lee, Sally, author.
Ankylosaurus / by Sally Lee.
pages cm. — (Smithsonian little explorer.
Little paleontologist)
Summary: "Introduces young readers to Ankylosaurus,
including physical characteristics, diet, habitat, life
cycle"— Provided by publisher.
Audience: Ages 4–7.
Audience: K to grade 3.
Includes index.
ISBN 978-1-4914-0808-7 (library binding)
ISBN 978-1-4914-0820-9 (paperback)
  ISBN 978-1-4914-0814-8 (paper over board)
    ISBN 978-1-4914-0826-1 (eBook PDF)
      1. Ankylosaurus—Juvenile literature.
      2. Dinosaurs—Juvenile literature. I. Title.
      QE862.O65L44 2015
      567.915—dc23   2014000451

Editorial Credits

Michelle Hasselius, editor; Heidi Thompson, designer;
Wanda Winch, media researcher; Kathy McColley,
production specialist

Our very special thanks to Mike Brett-Surman, PhD,
Museum Specialist for Fossil Dinosaurs, Reptiles,
Amphibians, and Fish at the National Museum of Natural
History, Smithsonian Institution, for his curatorial review.
Capstone would also like to thank Kealy Wilson, Product
Development Manager, and the following at Smithsonian
Enterprises: Ellen Nanney, Licensing Manager; Brigid
Ferraro, Vice President, Education and Consumer
Products; Carol LeBlanc, Senior Vice President, Education
and Consumer Products.

Image Credits

Capstone: James Field, 1, 16–17, 22–23, Steve Weston,
14 (inset); Corbis: Bettmann, 26 (top), Reuters/David
Mercado, 16 (inset), StockTrek Images/Mark Stephenson,
20 (inset); Corel, 17 (insets), 18 (top right); Witmer Lab,
Department of Biomedical Services, Ohio University, 27
(t); Dreamstime: Aprescindere, 9 (inset); iStockphotos:
photos_martYmage, 15 (inset); Jia Tse, 25; Jon Hughes,
cover, 8–9, 12–13, 14–15, 20–21; Mary Evans Picture
Library: Natural History Museum, 10–11, 24, 30–31;
Photo courtesy of Bill Cotter, worldsfairphotos.com,
28–29; Shutterstock: BACO, 4 (bus), Catmando, 2–3, 4–5
(bkgrnd), jennyt, 19 (t), jennyt, 19 (bl), Kjersti Joergenssen, 23
(inset), leonello calvetti, 4 (dino silhouette), 6–7, Michael
Rosskothen, 18 (bm, br), Nastya22, 11 (inset), reallyround,
5 (tr), Shahril KHMD, 19, (br), Sofia Santos, 18 (l, all),
Steffen Foerster, 5 (tl), T4W4, 4 (folder), The _Pixel,
26–27 (map)

Printed in the United States of America in Stevens Point, Wisconsin.
032014   008092WZF14

TABLE OF CONTENTS

name: Ankylosaurus

how to say it: ang-KEE-low-SAWR-us

when it lived: Cretaceous Period, Mesozoic Era

what it ate: plants

size: 20 to 36 feet (6 to 11 meters) long
4 to 5 feet (1.2 to 1.5 m) tall
weighed 4 to 5 tons
(3.6 to 4.5 metric tons)

Ankylosaurus was the tank of the dinosaur world.
This armored plant eater could stand up against
almost any hungry predator!

Thanks to FOSSILS

A fossil is evidence of life from the past. Fossils of things like bones, teeth, and tracks found in the earth have taught us everything we know about dinosaurs.

THE FUSED LIZARD

body covered with armored plates

armored skull, with a tiny brain

short neck

un-plated stomach

Ankylosaurus was one of the biggest of all armored dinosaurs. It belonged to a group of dinosaurs called the ankylosaurs.

Ankylosaurus's name means "fused lizard." Bones in its skull and other parts of its body grew together. This made Ankylosaurus's bones thick and strong.

strong upper legs

tail club

STRONG ARMOR

Ankylosaurus was built like an army tank. It was covered with plates of bone called osteoderms. The plates were attached to the dinosaur's tough, leathery skin.

osteoderms

armadillo

Osteoderms are also found on crocodiles, armadillos, and some lizards today.

Large osteoderms covered Ankylosaurus's shoulders and neck. Smaller plates and knobs fit in between them. They let Ankylosaurus move.

The only part of the dinosaur that didn't have armor was its stomach.

HARD SKULL

Ankylosaurus's skull was covered with thick armor and sharp horns. The horns were shaped like triangles. Two stuck out from each cheek. Two more horns protected the back of its head. Armor even protected Ankylosaurus's eyes.

Most dinosaurs had small brains for their size. But Ankylosaurus had one of the smallest.

The shape of Ankylosaurus's head shows that this dinosaur likely had a strong sense of smell. Ankylosaurus could use its nose to sniff out predators nearby.

The part of Ankylosarus's brain used for thinking was as small as a walnut.

TAIL CLUB

This tank of a dinosaur had a built-in weapon at the end of its tail. It was a heavy club made of fused bones.

Ankylosaurus had powerful muscles at the base of its tail. It could swing its deadly tail club back and forth, smashing anything it hit.

Ankylosaurus's tail bones were locked together to make a stiff support for the club.

Ankylosaurus had to have a sturdy tail. A floppy tail wouldn't have been able to hold up its 100-pound (45-kilogram) club.

SAFE FROM PREDATORS

Most predators left the adult Ankylosaurus alone.
Its size and strong armor made it too hard to kill.

A predator
would have to get
to Ankylosaurus's soft
stomach to kill it.
When in danger, Ankylosaurus
dropped to the ground to
protect its belly.

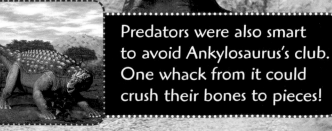

Predators were also smart
to avoid Ankylosaurus's club.
One whack from it could
crush their bones to pieces!

Ankylosaurus's great weight kept even strong Tyrannosaurus rex from flipping it over.

A porcupine also protects itself by lying on its belly.

ON THE MOVE

Ankylosaurus didn't have to run from predators.
But that doesn't mean it couldn't get moving
when it wanted to.

ankylosaur footprints

In 1996 scientists in South
America found trackways
made by some type of
ankylosaur. The footprints
were farther apart than
expected. That meant
the ankylosaur was walking
fast when the prints
were made.

Scientists use trackways to guess how fast Ankylosaurus could move. They think it could go as fast as 6 miles (9.7 kilometers) per hour.

Ankylosaurus's front legs were shorter than its back legs. This is similar to other dinosaurs, like Stegosaurus and Triceratops.

Stegosaurus   Triceratops

CRETACEOUS PERIOD

The conditions of the Cretaceous Period were just right for Ankylosaurus. The weather was warm and wet.

Other Cretaceous Animals

Tyrannosaurus rex

Triceratops

Utahraptor

Microraptor

Spinosaurus

The Cretaceous Period lasted from 145 to 66 million years ago.

DINOSAUR ERA

TRIASSIC | JURASSIC | CRETACEOUS

250   200   145   66   present

millions of years ago

Ankylosaurus ate flowering plants like magnolias and ficus. Plants grew faster during this time period. Plant-eating dinosaurs had more to eat. This may be one reason the Cretaceous Period had the biggest dinosaurs of all.

ficus

magnolia

DAILY LIFE

Ankylosaurus lived on a plain at the edge
of a shallow sea. It spent almost all of its
time eating and searching for food.

Peaceful
Ankylosaurus was
usually alone. With
its strong armor,
Ankylosaurus didn't
need a herd to
protect it.

Some scientists think Ankylosaurus made sounds through its nose. It did this to find a mate. It could also let another Ankylosaurus know it was hurt or in danger.

MEALTIME

Ankylosaurus was an herbivore. That means it ate plants. Because of its huge size, Ankylosaurus needed a lot of food.

Ankylosaurus couldn't lift its head very high. It had to eat plants close to the ground.

Ankylosaurus's small teeth couldn't do much chewing. It swallowed its food whole.

Ankylosaurus had a beak, like a turtle. Leaf-shaped teeth lined the sides of its jaws. Ankylosaurus used its beak to snip off the plants.

hawksbill turtle

EGGS AND BABIES

Ankylosaurus began life inside an egg smaller than a soccer ball. Its mother laid 20 to 30 eggs at a time. She probably did not stay to take care of her offspring.

Meat-eating predators killed most young dinosaurs. Very few lived to become adults.

A young Ankylosaurus didn't have enough armor to keep it safe. As it got older, its armor grew slowly from its head toward its tail.

Laying many eggs improved the chances of some Ankylosaurus offspring surviving to adulthood.

FIRST DISCOVERED

A team led by paleontologist Barnum Brown found the first Ankylosaurus bones in 1906. They were in Montana. The team found only part of a skull, a few bones, and plates.

Barnum Brown

Canada

Montana

Ankylosaurus is one of the best-known dinosaurs. But scientists have found only a few fossils to study. Only two skulls and parts of three skeletons have been found. No one has ever found a whole Ankylosaurus skeleton.

Brown didn't know Ankylosaurus had a club until 1910. That year he discovered a tail club in Canada.

Barnum Brown was one of the greatest fossil hunters of all time. He discovered many dinosaur bones, including the first Tyrannosaurus rex.

A FAMOUS ANKYLOSAURUS

Barnum Brown helped design an Ankylosaurus model before he died in 1963. He built it based on what scientists knew about Ankylosaurus at the time.

Brown's life-sized model of Ankylosaurus was built for the 1964 World's Fair in New York. It is still on display at a museum in Texas.

All Mesozoic dinosaurs were extinct by the end of the Cretaceous Period. Ankylosaurus was one of the last dinosaurs to become extinct.

But scientists know more now. An Ankylosaurus model built today would have smaller spikes on its sides. Its armor would be made of different sizes and shapes of osteoderms.

GLOSSARY

armor—bones, scales, and skin that some animals have on their bodies for protection

extinct—no longer living; an extinct animal is one that has died out, with no more of its kind

ficus—a shrubby tree in the fig family

fossil—evidence of life from the geologic past

fuse—to join together

herd—a large group of animals that lives and moves together

magnolia—a tree or large shrub with large, fragrant flowers

Mesozoic Era—the age of dinosaurs, which includes the Triassic, Jurassic, and Cretaceous periods; when the first birds, mammals, and flowers appeared

model—something that is made to look like a person, animal, or object

offspring—animals born to a set of parents

osteoderm—an armor plate made of bone that is set into the skin

paleontologist—a scientist who studies fossils

plain—a large, flat area of land with few trees

predator—an animal that hunts other animals for food

skull—the bones of the head and face that protect the brain, eyes, and ears

trackway—a set of footprints from long ago found in rocks

CRITICAL THINKING USING THE COMMON CORE

Ankylosaurus lived during the same time period as Tyrannosaurus rex. Describe two ways Ankylosaurus protected itself from this dinosaur and other predators. (Key Ideas and Details)

Scientists found trackways of an ankylosaur in 1996. What are trackways? What did scientists learn about ankylosaurs from these trackways? Use the text and glossary to help you with your answer. (Craft and Structure)

READ MORE

Gray, Susan H., *Ankylosaurus.* Introducing Dinosaurs. Mankato, Minn.: Child's World, 2010.

Matthews, Rupert. *World's Weirdest Dinosaurs.* Extreme Dinosaurs. Chicago: Heinemann Library, 2012.

Raatma, Lucia. *Ankylosaurus.* Dinosaurs. Ann Arbor, Mich.: Cherry Lake Pub., 2013.

INTERNET SITES

FactHound offers a safe, fun way to find Internet sites related to this book. All of the sites on FactHound have been researched by our staff.

Here's all you do:

Visit *www.facthound.com*

Type in this code: 9781491408087

Check out projects, games and lots more at
www.capstonekids.com

31

INDEX